JAZZ MASTERS

Thelonious Monk

JAZZ MASTERS

Thelonious Monk

by Stuart Isacoff

Amsco Publications
New York/London/Sydney

Cover design by Barbara Hoffman
Cover photo by Lee Tanner

Copyright © 1978 by Consolidated Music Publishers
Published 1987 by Amsco Publications,
A Division of Music Sales Corporation, New York, NY.

Order No. AM 19423
US International Standard Book Number: 0.8256.4080.6

Exclusive Distributors:
Music Sales Corporation
257 Park Avenue South, New York, NY 10010 USA
Music Sales Limited
8/9 Frith Street, London W1V 5TZ England
Music Sales Pty. Limited
120 Rothschild Street, Rosebery, Sydney, NSW 2018, Australia

Printed in the United States of America by
Vicks Lithograph and Printing Corporation

Contents

Thelonious Sphere Monk

(b. 1920)

In the early 1940s a small group of musicians would meet every Sunday afternoon at Milt Hinton's house to listen to records—mostly by Coleman Hawkins—and to talk about jazz. There was excitement and anticipation in the small room each week as Dizzy Gillespie, Ben Webster and Thelonious Monk gathered in search of new directions for their music. Something new was about to happen, a revolution in music called "bebop," and the conspiracy to spread it was spearheaded in that small Harlem flat.

It was not far from there that these giants of jazz would step up on the bandstand and create history. Their home base was Minton's, a club on 118th Street in Manhattan where sessions lasted through the night as musician after musician showed his stuff to the expectant audience. It was at Minton's that Monk and Dizzy began to work out complex chord substitutions to scare away the no-talents who tried to sit in. Soon, only Charlie Christian and a few others could keep up: "We are going to get a big band started," said Monk. "We're going to create something that they can't steal because they can't play it."

Over a decade later Monk's dream came true as he led a large orchestra in a Town Hall concert of his music. But the years between were harsh and bitter. Other musicians would call him "Mad Monk," and label his playing "zombie music." Dizzy faced similar problems, as when Cab Calloway told him to "stop playing that Chinese music in my band." But Monk, who was unable to work in New York City for ten years because he lost his cabaret card on a drug violation charge, was less able to fend for himself in the world.

Monk seemed not "present" unless he was actually talking to you, reported Minton's manager, Teddy Hill. Even then, Hill continued, he drifted away at times. One night Monk was found sitting in the kitchen writing music while the band was playing out front. He simply had not heard the group begin, so carried away was he with his creation. Monk lived for his music in those days, and there was little else to nourish him; there was nothing else he could do.

"I don't be around the corner, looking to see what's happening. I'm not a policeman or a social worker . . ." he told interviewer Valerie Wilmer. His domain was music, and he plunged into it with the abandon of a warrior. His sound developed from the solidity of the stride players, the quirkiness of the harmonic innovators, the percussive bounce of a new wave of drummers. It had the economy of a Japanese brush painting and the fullness of a rag-time stomp. It was angular and sweeping, with whole-tone scales and outrageous clusters.

whole – tone scale:

clusters:

It was endearing and humorous, and above all human.

Monk's influence is generally recognized as being limited to that of a composer. After all, his strange, seemingly technique-less way of playing has not achieved a vogue among later pianists. His close friend and favorite musician, Bud Powell, who approached the piano in a completely different manner, has unquestionably left a greater mark on the development of jazz piano style. But a closer look reveals a deep influence, especially on those who performed with him.

In those early days Monk recorded with many legendary musicians including Dizzy Gillespie, Charlie Parker, Coleman Hawkins and John Coltrane. (It was Monk who showed Trane how to play more than one note at a time on the saxophone.) "Working with Monk brought me close to a musical architect of the highest order," said John Coltrane. "I felt I learned from him in every way—sensually, theoretically, technically." "I learned a lot myself just listening to Monk play," said McCoy Tyner. "His concept of space alone was one of the most important things he taught Coltrane; when to lay out and let somebody else fill up that space, or just leave the space open. I think John was already going in that direction, but working with Monk helped him reach his goal that much faster."*

At present Monk is largely inactive, and he has been in declining health over the last several years. But his music and his legacy will influence countless musicians for years to come. Perhaps a key to Monk's greatness lies with the philosopher Plutarch: ". . . medicine, to produce health," he said," has to examine disease; music, to create harmony, must investigate discord."

* Thomas, J.C., *Chasin' the Trane*, N.Y.: Da Capo Press, Inc. page 84.

Off Minor

Thelonious Monk
Solo transcribed by Bob Himmelberger

Fast medium bounce

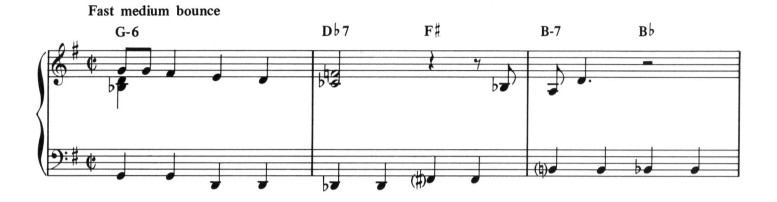

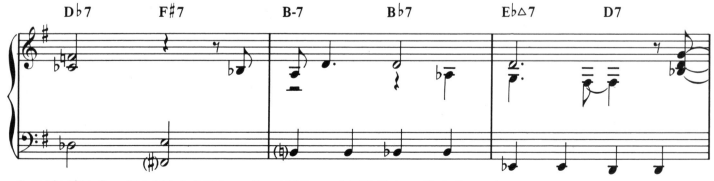

11

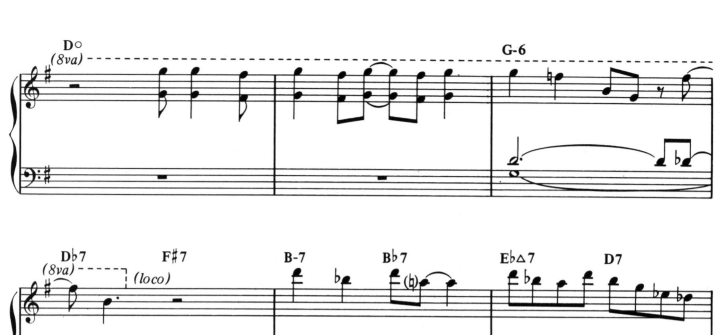

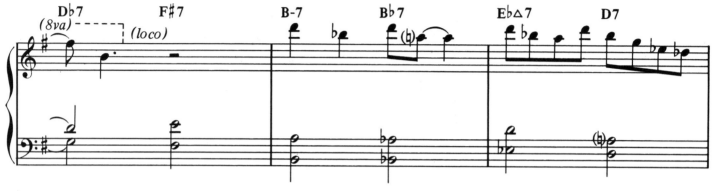

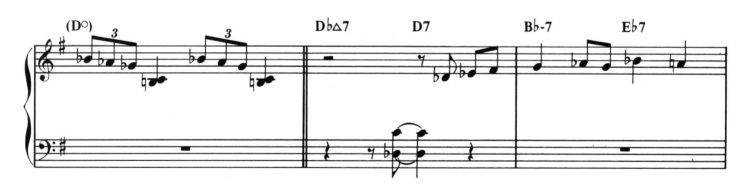

I Mean You

Thelonious Monk and Coleman Hawkins
Solo transcribed by Jerry Kovarsky

Medium bounce tempo

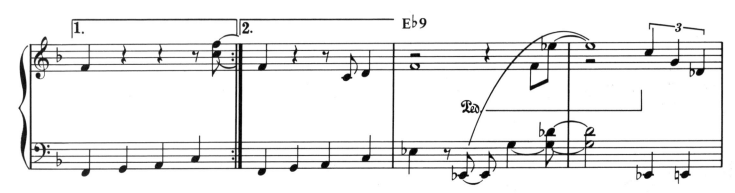

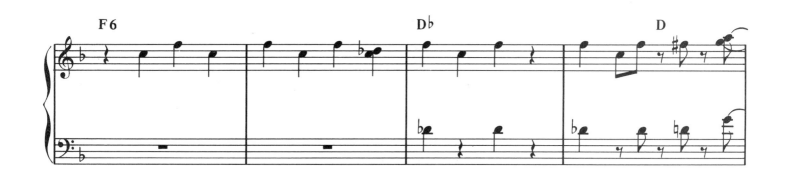

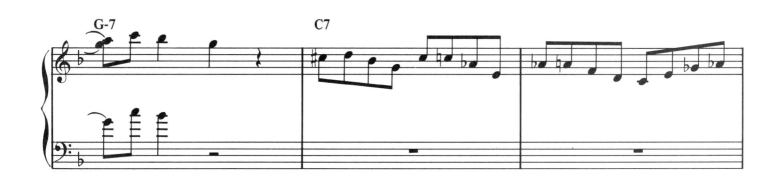

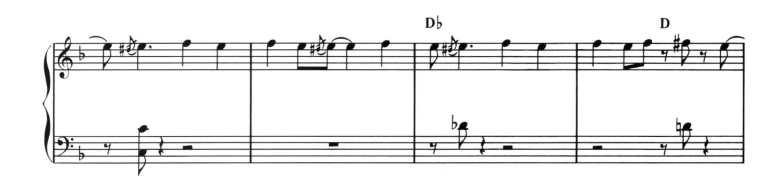

Ruby My Dear

Thelonious Monk
Solo transcribed by Bob Himmelberger

31

In Walked Bud

Thelonious Monk
Solo transcribed by Jerry Kovarsky

Medium fast tempo

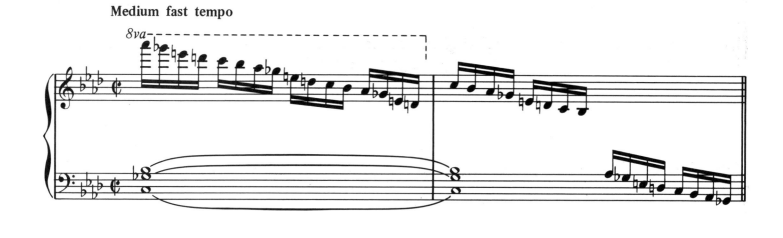

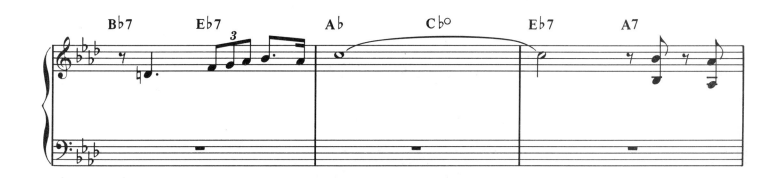

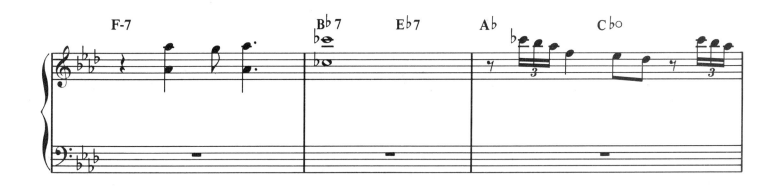

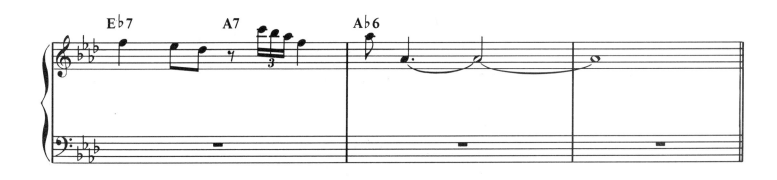

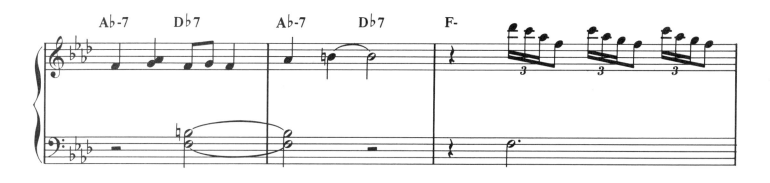

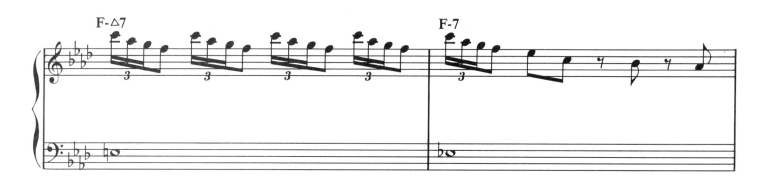

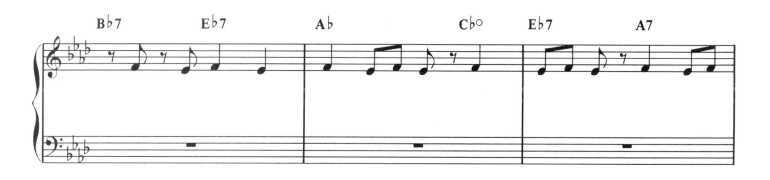

Monk's Mood

Thelonious Monk

Thelonious

Thelonious Monk
Solo transcribed by Bob Himmelberger

*Monk plays only the melody notes of this tune while the descending chordal movement is played by the horns.

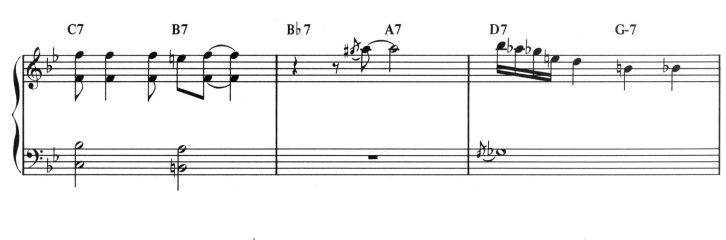

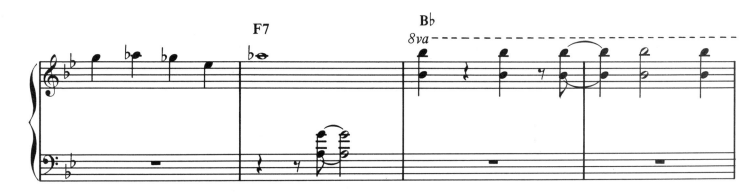

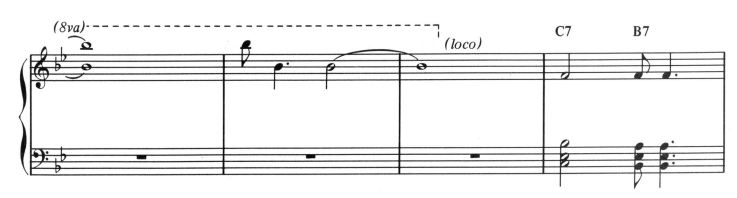

Epistrophy

Thelonious Monk and Kenneth S. Clarke
Solo transcribed by Stuart Isacoff

49

Introspection

Thelonious Monk
Solo transcribed by Jerry Kovarsky

Out of tempo

Relaxed medium-fast tempo

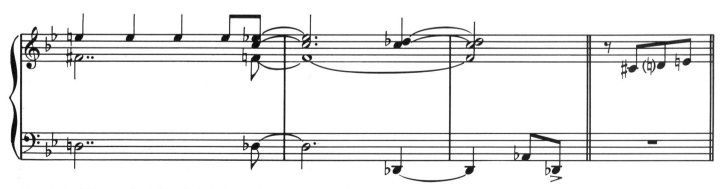

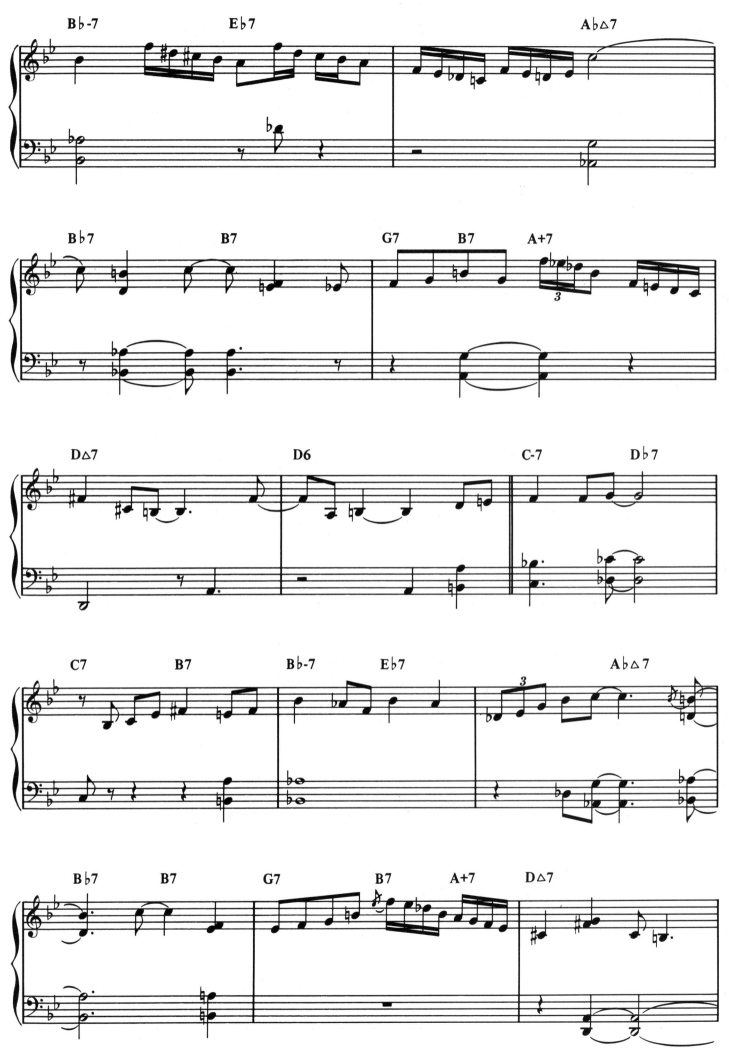

Discography

Tune	Album	
Ruby My Dear	*Thelonious Monk with John Coltrane*	Riverside JLP 46
Epistrophy	*Monk's Music*	Riverside RLP 12-242
Off Minor In Walked Bud Thelonious Introspection	*Genius of Modern Music Vol. I*	Blue Note 1510
Monk's Mood	*Genius of Modern Music Vol. II*	Blue Note 1511
I Mean You	*Thelonious Monk Big Band and Quartet in Concert*	Columbia CS 8964